W9-CEV-752

Some Kind of Lucky

A FIFTY-YEAR LOVE AFFAIR WITH MARTHA'S VINEYARD

Some Kind of Lucky

A FIFTY-YEAR LOVE AFFAIR WITH MARTHA'S VINEYARD

JOAN COWEN BOWMAN

Photos by ALISON SHAW

VINEYARD STORIES

Edgartown, Massachusetts

To my son, Bo, and to my family, and to all of us
who love the Island as passionately as he did.

Volume Copyright ©2014 Joan Cowen Bowman

Photos ©2014 Alison Shaw

Published by Vineyard Stories
52 Bold Meadow Road
Edgartown, Massachusetts 02539
508-221-2338
www.vineyardstories.com

All rights reserved. No part of this book may be reproduced or transmitted in any form or by any
means, electronic or mechanical, including photocopying, recording, or any other information
storage and retrieval system, without the written permission of the copyright owners.

Library of Congress Number: 2013956070
ISBN: 978-0-9849136-9-5

Book Design: Jill Dible, Atlanta, Georgia

Printed in China

3 4015 07140 6761

CONTENTS

INTRODUCTION ~ 9

The Magic
1. Some Kind of Lucky ~ 13
2. Island Dangers ~ 19
3. Vineyard Interrupted ~ 25
4. Homes away from Home ~ 31

My Quitsa Days
5. A Millennium Wedding ~ 39
6. Unexpected Gifts ~ 45
7. The Attack on America ~ 51
8. Another Riptide ~ 55

Saturday Mornings
9. Menemsha Dining ~ 63
10. A Bittersweet July ~ 69
11. Island Miracles ~ 75
12. More Island Miracles ~ 79

The Crossing
13. Heartbreak ~ 85
14. A Visitation ~ 93
15. Joyous Meals ~ 99

AFTERWORD: Hiding in Plain Sight ~ 105
AUTHOR BIOGRAPHY ~ 107

INTRODUCTION

JOAN COWEN BOWMAN, JANUARY 2014

Throughout my story, *Some Kind of Lucky*, I'm sharing at age eighty two the impact of the Vineyard on my life since I first came here for the summer months in 1962, recently divorced with four young children.

I describe how my sense of wonderment for the Island was honed during my childhood years on "The Place"—my grandparents' estate on the North Jersey Shore—where the enchanting surroundings there compensated for my loneliness and isolation: a rambling mansion with lavish gardens and greenhouses on ten acres of manicured property, filled with seasonal delights.

On the Vineyard I uncover different enchantments. Severed from the mainland, surrounded by water—the origin of life—the Vineyard offers me a simpler existence and a serenity that comes from being closer to nature. Not only is its natural beauty breathtaking, but its daily pace is also slower—making it possible to savor each day and each other. The Island seems to encourage intimate revelations that would not be forthcoming between us in our lives at home. There is also unlimited time to

read and to reflect. Even meals are simpler and fresher—with organic farms and farmers' markets nearby and fresh fish caught daily in local waters. Sunrise and moonrise, birdsong at dawn and dusk, the lullaby of the tides as we sleep—all these remind us throughout our days and nights that there is some kind of order in the universe.

Now, more than fitty summers have passed since I first discovered the Island. In my story I describe ongoing joys and sorrows—merry family reunions, festive weddings, bitter divorces, unexpected deaths. I describe how the Island has given me a stronger sense of freedom and self-reliance, opened up my feelings, brought me closer to my family, and enhanced my skills as a writer. I relate how the Vineyard never ceases to surprise me with its serendipitous happenings, and how its healing powers have continued to rescue and renew me from the emotional turmoil surrounding my everyday life on the mainland.

I fervently hope that *Some Kind of Lucky* resonates with readers who, like myself and my family, return year after year to this sanctuary in the sea that we all love beyond reason.

The Magic

D0101500

At home in New Jersey, friends and acquaintances who have never visited Martha's Vineyard ask me why I have returned to this Island with my family, again and again, over fifty years. "What is it about the place?" they inevitably ask. / "Life is simpler there," I try to explain. "It restores my spirit. It's a healing place. And most of the time I don't have to wear shoes." / I don't tell them that crossing over Vineyard Sound on the ferry from Woods Hole I can palpably feel all the stress induced by my hectic life "in America"—as year-round Vineyarders ironically refer to the mainland—slowly draining away. / I don't wax poetic about the fiery sunsets over the Chilmark hills, the eerie hush of Menemsha harbor in the fog, the Milky Way quilting the sapphire night skies over Stonewall Beach. / And I also don't tell them that I come here for the magic. . . .

1. SOME KIND OF LUCKY / 1961

On a gray, windblown Saturday afternoon in November 1961 I'm driving reluctantly to "The Place," the estate on the North Jersey Shore— an hour away from my own home in northern New Jersey—where my brother, Tommy, and I spent our childhoods. The rambling, white clapboard mansion on ten acres of parklike land was built in 1906 by my grandfather, Clarence J. Houseman, and his wife, Flora, in West End, a section of Long Branch—a famous summer resort at the time—and my parents still live there.

I'm almost thirty years old and recently divorced. A college romance led to an unexpected pregnancy and a hasty wedding after my graduation from Smith College in 1954. Four children and six years later, miserable in my marriage, I fought for my freedom against my family's wishes. Now I was a divorcée living in suburbia: the phrase "single parent" had not yet entered our vocabulary. I love being a mother to my three sons, Ricky, Jimmy, and Teke, and my daughter, Lisa—little steps ages two to six—and I'm relieved that my battle for independence from my husband is over. But socially I feel freakish and isolated; I'm definitely in a reclusive mode.

Driving south on the Garden State Parkway, I reflect on the history of "The Place"—embedded in my consciousness from the stories my mother told me over and over when I was a child. She was only three years old when her father—a self-made millionaire by the 1890s—built the house as a summer home and named the estate "The Homestead," which refers to a house with

At home in New Jersey, 1962, Teke, Jimmy, Lisa and Ricky

adjoining buildings and land. The mansion was complete with seven airy bedrooms, each with its own bathroom—a veritable luxury in those days—and an expansive servants' wing, a warren of tiny rooms, fully occupied. The property boasted stables, greenhouses, a gardener's cottage, lavish flower and vegetable gardens, a charming rose garden, a lily pond, and a gazebo—all carefully tended by a flock of workers, for help was inexpensive and plentiful during the early decades of the twentieth century.

When my mother inherited the estate after Clarence's death in 1931, she and my father, recently married, decided to live there year-round. My father, nine years older than my mother, was thirty-nine when they married. Born in 1893, he graduated from Princeton in 1913, the youngest in his class. He served as a lieutenant in the artillery during World War I, and—by the time he met and married my mother—was successfully guiding the Wall Street firm he had founded in the 1920s, Cowen and Company, through the Great Depression. My mother told me often how she adored "The Homestead" and also adored my father; she also shared that he had never wanted children. Nevertheless, I was born in 1932; my brother,

Tommy, in 1934; and we grew up adoring the estate just as my mother did.

As far back as I can remember I always thought of the mansion and the property as "The Place," rather than "The Homestead." And during my childhood, before I left for boarding school in 1946, I was familiar with every inch of the house and its surrounding ten acres. No matter what season of the year, I loved all its sounds and colors and smells and tastes. Even though my parents' bedroom was far away down the upstairs hall and they didn't always seem to care about me, instead hiring outsiders to attend to my needs—cooks, maids, governesses—they couldn't take my very own special kingdom away from me. I never heard the words, "I love you, Joan!" or even, "What a pretty little girl you are, Joan!" But "The Place" wrapped its arms around me—nurtured me and made me feel safe.

Although my brother, Tommy, and I had each lived independently after our college years, "The Place" continued to dominate our lives. My parents loved to entertain, and we returned there often—always for Thanksgiving and Christmas as well as for certain birthdays and other celebrations. On this particular Saturday, Tommy—now twenty-seven and a

bachelor living in Manhattan—is hosting his biennial Brown-Princeton cocktail party on "The Place" after the football game at Palmer Stadium on the Princeton campus. And I'm dreading the evening ahead.

To put it simply, I'm not feeling very lucky about my life, and I'm certainly not in the mood for a cocktail party filled with boisterous, single, twenty-somethings. But a man named Peter approaches me soon after I walk into the noisy, smoke-filled living room, and we hit it off. He is tall, dark, and handsome, divorced with no children, and trying to break into the advertising world in New York City. Before long we're dating.

Peter's maiden aunt is a resident of Martha's Vineyard and the proprietor of the Shetland Shop in Vineyard Haven—a charming boutique off Beach Road, within walking distance of the ferry, that sells imported Scottish woolen goods. (It's now Budget Rent-a Car.) At that time, in the early sixties, most people had never heard of the Vineyard, or if they had—like me before I met Peter—they thought it was part of Cape Cod.

"I've got to get you to the Island," he keeps telling me during the early months of our romance. "It's the perfect summer place for you and the four kids. I know you'll fall in love with it."

Over Easter the following spring, when my children are spending the holiday weekend with their father and his parents in Washington, D.C., Peter and I visit his aunt Kate on the Island. As he predicted, I'm enchanted and rent my first house there that summer of 1962.

It's an old sea captain's house, a simple home of weathered shingles near the Gay Head Light on the most westerly tip of the Island, isolated and sea-swept. The rent is one hundred dollars per week. The living room faces the Atlantic, and from the picture window the limitless sea seems to stretch all the way to Spain. Behind the house, through a thicket of wild blueberry bushes, an ancient Indian graveyard, reputedly haunted, stands on a knoll. At night, the lighthouse, perched on top of the nearby cliffs, flashes its beacon through our bedroom windows—guarding me and my family, it seems, as well as the ships at sea.

My hopes for a healthy, healing July and August with the four children—away from my brokenhearted ex-husband, my angry parents, my former in-laws who aren't speaking to me—are more than fulfilled. Although Peter is very attentive and has serious intentions, I know I am not in love with him; our romance is short-lived. My love affair with the Island, however, turns out to be long-lasting. The Vineyard and its lore get under my skin during that first two-month stay and have been part of my life ever since.

My second marriage in 1967 brings two more sons, Bo and Jonathan, into the family. But my gifted, charismatic, and—as it turns out—relentlessly self-destructive husband feels no special warmth for the Vineyard. Eventually, however, when I find my way back to the Island, Bo and Jonathan also fall under its spell.

So in 1961 I go to a party I don't really want to go to and meet a man I don't fall in love with and choose not to marry. But he cares for me deeply and leads me to an island in the sea that has altered and enriched my life—and the lives of my six children and ultimately their own children—forever.

Now, isn't that some kind of lucky?

The Vineyard and its lore get under my skin during that first two-month stay and have been part of my life ever since.

2. ISLAND DANGERS / 1962–1963

Sea, sand, and sky surround our lives that first summer of 1962. Sunny days on the beaches blend into each other as the weeks go by. On our Gay Head Beach the four children climb the cliffs and fashion fanciful bowls and sculptures from the clay; at Menemsha Beach there are friendly fishermen to visit on the jetty and slippery squid to catch from the dock. On gray days, the Flying Horses Carousel in Oak Bluffs beckons. On our way we always stop to feed the family of swans at Mill Pond in West Tisbury.

Visitors find us in our remote, westerly outpost. Peter, my brother, Tommy, and his new bride, Connie, even my parents come for a long weekend. Friends from down-Island come for the day.

"Wow!" A couple exclaims when they arrive at the house after a forty-five-minute drive from East Chop. "You really wanted to get away from it all this summer!"

Our guests do not disrupt our tranquil, untroubled existence. Day after day, the children are happy, and I am finding serenity. Island life is everything I hoped for.

Halfway through our two-month stay in Gay Head, however, we also learn that the Island is not without its dangers. One afternoon we come back to the house to discover that Teke's little red sneakers have been left behind at Menemsha Beach, eight miles away. My summer helper, Roberta, a reliable high-school girl from New Jersey, insists on driving back to Menemsha to retrieve the sneakers, and Teke, now almost three years old, wants to go along for the ride.

The Gay Head roads are narrow and curving; Roberta swerves to avoid a driver coming toward her from the opposite direction and plows into a telephone pole. Teke is thrown violently against the dashboard (years before the invention of seat belts and airbags); he spends three days in the Martha's Vineyard Hospital with a concussion and a broken leg. My station wagon is totaled, as is the telephone pole. Fortunately, my insurance company agrees to replace both. There are no automobile dealerships on the Island; I pick Teke up at the hospital in a creaky, old rental Jeep that guzzles quarts of oil daily. We drive around the Island in it for ten days to the delight of all four kids; they are sorely disappointed when my shiny new station wagon is delivered from the mainland and I have to turn in the jalopy.

Teke's accident, however, does not dim our enthusiasm for the Island; the children can't wait to return the following summer. July 1963 finds us in a snug farmhouse on South Road in Chilmark—not far from Beetlebung Corner—where the four of them can race out the door every morning for games and fun at the Community Center nearby. We rent there for several years, for the most part a calm, carefree time.

But one afternoon during our first summer in the farmhouse, the surf is kicking up after a storm has passed through in the night. Ricky and Jimmy are eager to ride the waves at Squibnocket Beach. They don't last long in the water; it's too much for them. Lisa, not yet six, has barely mastered the dog paddle but is begging to go in. One of my Smith 1954 classmates is visiting for a few days. (Jane and I are members of the Rowdy Crew—a handful of boisterous, irreverent freshmen who received that moniker from our housemother during our first semester on the Northampton campus.) We're both strong swimmers, and we decide to accommodate Lisa's pleas and give it a try.

The waves are enormous and crashing; with Lisa in tow, we quickly realize we will have to get out beyond where they are breaking, where the water is deep but calm. At first we're relieved to be beyond the turmoil of the heavy surf, where Lisa can paddle around on her own—even though the water is way over our heads. But our relief is temporary. Before we know it, we are being pulled out to sea by an invisible riptide. The beach, the cliffs beyond it, and the other bathers on shore (no one else is in the water) are receding from our vision, becoming smaller and smaller as we are pulled out farther and farther. I can barely make out three orange dots on the shoreline—the brightly

On the dock at Menemsha, July 1963. Lisa, Teke, Jimmy, Ricky

colored hooded sweatshirts that I bought Lisa's brothers earlier that summer so that they are easy to spot when I come to pick them up at the beach or on the jetty at Menemsha.

We decide to start swimming back against the undertow. It's rough going for me; I'm hampered with Lisa under one arm. Jane swims strongly a few yards in front of me. We're still far from the towering waves that separate us from safety on shore. I'm beginning to panic, and I suddenly know that I don't have the strength to make it on my own with Lisa in tow. The water is still above our heads, and I sense that I will need more than my stamina alone—if I have any left—to get her through that barrier of crashing surf to safety on the other side. If a wave wrenches her from my grasp, I fear that she will be dragged back out to sea and lost forever.

I cry out to Jane, still a few strokes ahead of me, "Don't leave! Stay back with me and help!" Jane turns around and swims back to join us.

Swimming side by side with Lisa still in my grasp, Jane and I approach the wall of waves, agreeing to take turns. The first wave pounds down on Lisa and me; she is torn from my arms. Jane and I, thrashing around in surf still over our heads, come up for air, desperately looking for Lisa. Finding her nearby, Jane grabs

her, and the scenario repeats itself with each oncoming wave as we get closer to shore. Finally, with Lisa in tow again, grappling with what I hope is the last wave before safety on land, I lose her once more in the turbulent surf. When I surface I see Jane on her knees in shallow water with Lisa clinging to her. I watch as they limp onto the sand.

Knowing that Lisa is safe, I give myself over to the now shallow incoming tide, letting the water push me over the bank of sand at shoreline like a piece of driftwood. My ankles are bleeding from the small stones and rocks that banged against my feet in my struggles with the surf; mucus is dripping from my nose and mouth. I'm shaking so hard from fear and exhaustion I can't even stand up.

We end up about fifty yards farther down the beach from where we first waded into the sea. The boys, who have been following our travails, are waiting for us there at water's edge—three little worried faces framed by their orange hoods. Slowly I pull myself together to make my way back down the beach to where we had started. The tide is coming in, and the wind has picked up; Squibnocket has certainly lost its allure for that particular afternoon. We pack up the cooler and beach towels and drive back to our cozy farmhouse—Jane and myself for a stiff Scotch. I know that without her I probably would have lost my only daughter. The kids—including Lisa—are nonplussed about the incident. They're too young to understand that it has been a near-drowning. But Jane and I, despite our swimming prowess, never feel quite the same way about the ocean after that.

Has the Island, my newly adopted refuge, briefly betrayed me on this traumatic afternoon at Squibnocket during our second summer? I don't think of Lisa's near-drowning as a betrayal. Instead, it makes me aware that, despite my strength and stamina, I'm extremely vulnerable to the capriciousness of the natural world—to arbitrary, terrifying happenings that are totally out of my control.

This awareness stands in sharp contrast to the benign world that surrounded me during my childhood. Nature on "The Place"—with its manicured gardens, gazebos, and greenhouses—was tamed and cultivated. The infrequent arrival of a blizzard or hurricane was actually exciting to me as a child, not threatening. "The Place," my childhood refuge, was impregnable, a bastion of safety and security.

But on the Vineyard, that summer of 1963, I'm awakened to the duality of nature—and I gain a new respect and awe for not only its precarious, delicate beauty but also its raw, unpredictable powers.

I gain a new respect and awe for not only [the Vineyard's] precarious, delicate beauty but also its raw, unpredictable powers.

3. VINEYARD INTERRUPTED / 1964-1967

In New Jersey a few months later in mid-November 1963, I find myself back on "The Place"—once again attending Tommy's Brown-Princeton cocktail party, held every other year after the Saturday afternoon football game at Palmer Stadium. Despite the riptide incident—or perhaps because of it—my second summer on the Vineyard has given me a stronger sense of myself. I'm feeling more self-confident and less self-conscious than two years ago—more comfortable in my own skin. I'm actually looking forward to the get-together.

Once again, the living room is filled with familiar people smoking, drinking, chatting—my brother's friends from Brown and various wives and dates. Across the crowded room I notice my parents talking to a rugged young man I have never seen before. My attraction to him is intense and immediate. I feel a magnetic pull and weave my way through the guests to be introduced.

Mike Bowman—a legendary Princeton football captain—is a carefree thirty-year-old bachelor when I meet him in the living room on "The Place"; I'm a thirty-two-year-old divorcée with four children. He is gifted, charismatic, popular—a big bear of a man, full of tall stories and bon mots—with a huge circle of friends and acquaintances. He refers to our relationship, with a laugh, as a "sociological nightmare." "Opposites attract because they have so much in common," he loves to tell me, with a twinkle in his eyes. And there is no question that we are powerfully attracted to one another, on every level.

Mike is of Anglo-Irish heritage and was

raised in a broken, impoverished family in the outskirts of Boston. He worked his way through Princeton on scholarship—the first member of his blue-collar family to attend college. His legendary accomplishments and charismatic personality fascinate me. He also has a dark, moody side, but I choose to overlook his unstable behavior; I become completely addicted to him, and I believe he adores me. I think of him as the love of my life; I think we have everything. I am also in rescuer mode, trusting that I can give him everything he has never had—a faithful wife, a stable home, a loving family.

By the time we marry four years later, Mike has embarked on a meteorically successful career on Wall Street. My hopes for a happy, fulfilling marriage to the man of my dreams are now under way. I believe I have chosen a loving husband, an attentive stepfather, and a proud father-to-be for our future children. By February 1972 our first son, Michael Jr. (nicknamed Bo), is three years old, and our second son, Jonathan (nicknamed Jon), is born that month on Leap Year Day.

As the early years of our marriage evolve, however, Mike's behavior continues to be unpredictable and unstable. The sporadic moodiness that I was aware of during our courtship still prevails at times; at other times he's bursting with charm and energy, almost manic. He is extremely focused on building his career on Wall Street, which includes entertaining clients after work well into the evening hours; some nights he doesn't return home or even call to let me know his whereabouts. He has a sweet side, and I believe him when he consoles me, telling me how much he loves me and that we share something special. In the meantime, his successes as an institutional salesman and trader are becoming legendary, camouflaging his dark side to the outside world.

—◦—

Mike does not share my enthusiasm for the Vineyard. It's a nuisance to get to; the weather there is unpredictable; the *New York Times* and the *Wall Street Journal* are overpriced and not available early enough each morning. A meat-and-potatoes man, he isn't thrilled with our daily regime of pastas, fresh fish, and organic vegetables either. But at his suggestion, in the summer of 1978—when our sons Bo and Jonathan are nine and six—we rent a house in Chilmark for ten days. Perhaps he is trying to

My family on Quansoo, August 1987

please me; perhaps he just wants to give the Island another try—he never explains. A spate of overcast weather, however, reinforces his dislike of the place.

Eight years later, in 1986, when Bo graduates from the Trinity-Pawling School, he and seven other classmates rent a house in Vineyard Haven for the summer. I fly up for a long weekend with Jonathan, then fourteen; we drive around in our rental car, revisiting each one of the seven distinctive communities that dot the twenty-mile-long Island. As we find favorite haunts that we remember from our earlier trip in 1978 and discover new ones, we keep asking ourselves why we have waited so long to return to such a captivating place.

In the meantime, Mike's dark side has gradually taken over our marriage. Haunted by profound, unacknowledged feelings of worthlessness, his "moodiness" slowly spirals into a vortex of intense depression and self-destruction. By the time of Bo's graduation, I'm convinced that I need to ask him to leave and try to stabilize his life—still hoping I can both resurrect the gifted, charismatic man I had fallen in love with and also save our marriage.

Not able to rely on Mike and his judgments, I'm making more and more decisions for the family independently. After Jonathan and I visit Bo and happily rediscover the Island, I decide to approach the four older children—who have graduated from college and are now living all over the country—about a rental there for a month the following summer. All of them are intrigued with the idea of a family reunion on the Vineyard if I rent for the month of August in 1987. My daughter, Lisa, and I meet on the Island in October 1986 to search for a house.

We choose a contemporary home on Quansoo, just over the Chilmark line. Several miles down a bumpy dirt road, the rental stands on a flat point of land dotted with scrub oak, adjacent to Black Point, a gorgeous stretch of gated, private beach. On August 19 the following summer, I celebrate my fifty-fifth birthday there—surrounded by all six children. We are all thrilled to be back on the Island. Mike—who moved out the previous fall at my request and has been working on his problems through AA and intensive psychotherapy—is also on hand, desperately trying to win me back and return to the family.

After a hiatus of twenty-three years, our annual summer stays on the Vineyard have begun again.

After a hiatus of twenty-three years, our annual summer stays on the Vineyard have begun again.

4. HOMES AWAY FROM HOME / 1988–1999

On a cold, clear weekend in the winter of 1988, Bo and I fly up to the Vineyard together to choose a different rental, this time for the coming month of July. I'm determined to return with my family—not back to Quansoo, but further up-Island to Chilmark, where the landscape of rolling hills, ancient stone walls, and old shingled houses speaks to me and warms my heart.

Mike moved back in with me soon after our month on Quansoo in August 1987; I'm hopeful that we can work things out. He seems sober and stable and dedicated to the family. He also knows how much my rediscovery of the Vineyard means to me and all the children; he does not try to deter me from my ongoing summer plans.

Bo and I stay overnight at the Charlotte Inn in Edgartown; after a delicious dinner in the main house we leave to find our bedrooms in the annex across the way. South Summer Street is empty of cars and pedestrians. A gentle snow is falling; a hundred years fade away. I walk into a Currier and Ives lithograph and even imagine the clip-clop of a horse-drawn sleigh approaching down Main Street.

The next day Bo talks me into renting an eighteenth-century converted barn nestled in the Chilmark hills. Filled with reconstituted attic furniture and musty odors, the bargain rental price is its only redeeming feature. When we arrive on the first of July, however, Bo's prescient winter choice pleases me enormously. Breezes waft through the open doors and windows of the house, and in the summer light the furniture is endowed with a certain shabby-chic charm.

Carol's niece Ashley with my grandchildren Jovi, Jasper and Sheyna at Carol and Jim's wedding, July 1994

The two-hundred-year-old house, its shingles weathered by the sea air, sits on a small knoll on Quitsa Lane, just off South Road in rural Chilmark; it's only five miles from the old sea captain's house in Gay Head where I spent my first summer in 1962. Meandering stone walls frame the property; goldfinches dart from tree to tree; a pair of red-tailed hawks is usually in residence. The front porch, with its beckoning hammock, offers astounding views over connecting saltwater ponds to the quaint old fishing village of Menemsha and beyond, across Vineyard Sound. Below the porch at the foot of the front lawn is the ancient, weather-beaten tombstone of a member of the old Mayhew family—original seventeenth-century settlers—who died at sea. Legend has it that he was a victim of smallpox and was not allowed burial in the community cemetery for fear of contagion.

Inside the Barn, a bright, cheery kitchen has an oval oak pedestal table at one end for dining; the adjoining living room is furnished with sisal rugs, an old Boston rocker, and wing chairs and sofas covered in the pale blues of cotton duck and denim. An old trunk filled with rainy-day games serves as a coffee table. The original barn beams create a cozy loft upstairs that offers a twin bed; a large airy bedroom and a hall bathroom complete the second floor. The house has a cozy, thrown-together look, charming and quirky but not "decorated."

Outside the kitchen door across a small deck is the Tower, a smaller, more contemporary two-story structure also of weathered shingle, housing the master bedroom and a guest room. At night with the windows open I can hear the distant surf pulling in and out, an incessant, gentle lullaby.

I return to that house on Quitsa for six consecutive Julys—until 1994, when I need a larger rental for my son Jim's wedding weekend. He has stayed on in California after graduating from Stanford in 1987; his bride-to-be, Carol, fell under the Island's spell when visiting the previous summer of 1993. Unwilling to interrupt their work schedule in Los Angeles, they suggest that Lisa and I find a house for them in Chilmark; their one request is that they be married with a view of the sea.

In the meantime, despite ongoing therapy, AA, rehab programs, and eventually an extended stay in a psychiatric facility two hundred miles away, Mike has been unable to hold on to his stability since returning to the family in 1987. By Christmas of 1993 he has

been out of work for six years and, severely depressed, has given up actively looking for another job. When my son Bo comes home for the holidays he takes a fresh look at what is going on—and has been going on for some time.

"Put yourself first, Mom," he tells me. "You never have."

Bo's words inspire me to finally focus on rescuing myself, not my husband. I need to reclaim my life. I sense that Mike will make it extremely difficult for me, but I'm counting on my innate tenacity and resilience to see me through—as it had when I fought to end my first marriage and fought the riptide to save Lisa from drowning.

I have just started battling for my second divorce in January 1994 when Lisa and I

fly up to the Island to choose a house for the July wedding celebration. After many transcontinental phone calls, we settle on a large contemporary on a barren Chilmark hill with a view of the ocean. It's a bleak, overcast winter day, with the gray sky and the smoky sea melting into each other on the horizon. The home is lacking in charm, but its huge wraparound deck is perfect for the reception at one end, followed by dinner and dancing at the other. We return in July to unexpected Island magic. From the deck, the ocean sparkles in the summer sunlight; the front lawn, where the ceremony will take place, is encircled by a sea of gaily colored wildflowers; an old chestnut stallion grazes peacefully in the rolling fields next door.

Mike refuses to attend the wedding. "I wouldn't be caught dead there," he tells our housekeeper back home in New Jersey. But he also refuses to move out. Over the next thirteen months—enraged that I have the audacity to abandon him and also terrified of being alone—he digs in his heels and refuses to leave. We are polarized, living under the same roof but barely speaking to one another. The lawyers on both sides negotiate. Eventually, in February 1995 the divorce is granted; the terms for me are harsh. The court—through psychiatric and vocational evaluations—has found Mike completely dysfunctional and unemployable. I am ordered to support him financially, not only for the rest of his life, but also after my death. Should I predecease him, my estate will continue his monthly alimony payments; I will be paying him, so to speak, from my grave.

I'm sixty-three and Mike is sixty-one when he moves out. He never speaks to me—or my four older children from my first marriage—again. But even though we are completely estranged, his toxic aura hovers around me—exacerbated by the monthly alimony reminder on my bank statements, and by Bo and Jonathan's accounts of his irrational demands and misanthropic attitudes. I have broken my addiction, but I am still haunted by him.

Over the years, the man of my dreams has gradually turned into a monster, but each summer, the Island continues to wrap its arms around me and restore me. I stay on in the contemporary house with the expansive deck for two more years—welcoming my children and grandchildren and various friends—then return happily in July 1997 to my funky Barn and Tower on Quitsa Lane.

The Island continues
to wrap its arms around
me and restore me.

My Quitsa Days

H ere on Quitsa I really can live one day at a time; sometimes just one hour at a time. If I wake up to what my family calls a PVD—a Perfect Vineyard Day—my biggest decision will be which beach to go to; if it's damp and rainy I choose between wandering through my favorite galleries and shops or staying home wrapped up in the hammock with a new, coveted book. Later on, I'll drive to the organic farm for fresh-picked, thrice-washed lettuces, then on to the fish market for lobsters still swimming in their tank, or a slab of swordfish or striped bass, all from Vineyard waters. / In the late afternoon I like to go out the back door to walk down the dusty lane lined with honeysuckle and beach plum and rambling roses. Across the moors toward the sea, other old cottages of weathered shingle are nestled in the hilly landscape. At the end of the road, a winding, well-worn, uphill path traverses a thicket and suddenly emerges at the edge of a jagged cliff. A breathtaking panorama of the south shore comes into view, as luminous as a Winslow Homer painting. Down a steep wooden staircase a dream beach stretches away, its sands spotted with dark, glacial rocks, humped like whales. / Time stands still; the centuries melt away. I think of all the Wampanoag natives, the Portuguese sailors, the English settlers who have stood on this bluff long before me, harboring their hopes and dreams. I think of the Mayhew family that farmed this property in the seventeenth and eighteenth centuries, mourning the loss of a son who died at sea, burying his remains, which still rest—hundreds of years later—in the shelter of an ancient stone wall nearby. / An hour has passed. I walk back to the Barn to start dinner for my visiting family.

5. A MILLENNIUM WEDDING / 2000

My son Jonathan and I have been driving all day from New Jersey. Now, basking on the ferry deck in the sunshine, sharing an ice-cold beer—my station wagon, packed for the month, safely stowed below—we're talking about how different this July promises to be from previous ones. Our annual family reunion will be incorporated into a wedding weekend, and I am not returning to my rental on Quitsa Lane.

It's July 1 of the millennium year—and my son Teke, now in his last days as a forty-year-old bachelor, is getting married to Kristie, twenty-five, a beautiful Texan of Mexican heritage who fell under the Island's spell when she first visited a year ago. The wedding for ninety guests requires more space both inside and out than the house and property on Quitsa can provide. Instead, I've rented a big, airy

four-bedroom home at sea level on Stonewall Beach, with breathtaking views along the jagged shoreline from almost every window; ancient stone walls frame the expansive lawn where the wedding ceremony will take place, overlooking the sea.

At dinner together on our first evening on the Island, Kristie, Teke, Jonathan, and I review the wedding plans. The celebration weekend—still a week away—will start with a Friday evening clambake and finish with a farewell Sunday brunch at the house behind the Allen Farm that Teke and Kristie have rented for their honeymoon. Family and friends are coming from all over the country. Three members of the Rowdy Crew from my Smith days are staying in the house with me, always ready to pitch in and help out when needed. My brother,

Tommy; his wife, Connie; and their two married children, Todd and Jennifer, are arriving; my first husband, Red, now between his fourth and fifth marriages, is coming from New York City; his brother Kin is flying in from California. Greg and Erica, Red's two children from his second marriage, are also joining us. Everybody wants to come to a wedding on the Vineyard!

Both Kristie's parents are attending, but since a bitter divorce thirteen years ago, her mother has refused to speak to her father. Her paternal grandparents are also flying in from Texas; they still speak Spanish to each other at home, thirty miles south of San Antonio. A handful of her cousins and aunts from the Dallas area are also coming. Kristie is stressed with only a few days to go—worried about everyone getting along, about her hairdresser being on time, about the weather.

The whole mix could be a disaster. Nevertheless, I tell Kristie, "Don't worry about a thing." Remembering Jim and Carol's wedding six years earlier, I assure her, "The Island always weaves its magic."

I can tell from the bleak look in her gorgeous brown eyes that she doesn't believe me. And I don't tell her that I feel just as stressed as she does.

A week later—on Thursday morning—I wake up early to a crimson sunrise, followed by deep blue skies overhead. The air is dry and warm; temperatures rise to the high seventies by noon. I'm relieved when I hear from my neighbors that fair weather is predicted through Sunday.

Wedding guests start showing up for the weekend; a friend from New York City arrives with her car on an afternoon ferry. I give her explicit directions to our Chilmark house. She calls a half hour later on her cell phone. "I'm hung up on a rock on Stonewall Road," she announces with a nervous giggle. Jonathan and I rush up the road in our car to help. The "rock" turns out to be a large boulder; the wheels of her Nissan are suspended over it; the car is immobilized. I can't help asking myself, Is this a harbinger of the weekend to come?

By Friday afternoon the big white tent has been assembled on the front lawn, its three peaks silhouetted against the cloudless azure sky. At five-thirty, our ninety guests start arriving for the clambake. For an hour we sip drinks and munch hors d'oeuvres, mixing and mingling while admiring the astonishing view along the shoreline all the way to the Gay Head cliffs.

Kristie and Teke after the ceremony on Stonewall, July 8, 2000

My classmate Mildred (aka Mud)—one of the Rowdy Crew— is regaling Kristie's mother, sister, and cousins with stories from her Catholic girlhood; Kristie's father has Teke and his friends mesmerized with tales from his years on the Dallas police force.

Without warning, an enormous dark cloud appears out of nowhere over the house; I am struck by its peculiar shape, which resembles a whale. A few large raindrops fall. "Just passing over," the bartender assures me. Moments later, a violent squall envelops us with high winds and torrential rain. We rush to the tent and quickly roll down the sides to ward off the gale. The platters are ready, buffet-style, overflowing with seafood and barbecued chicken and corn on the cob. I move from table to table, showing the Texans how to dissect a lobster, coaxing them to try a steamed mussel or clam from the little mesh bag accompanying the lobster on each serving. There's high festivity in the air. Suddenly, the storm stops, the skies clear, and arcing up to the heavens, a magnificent double rainbow forms a huge semicircle over the horizon. Everyone rushes outside the tent in the middle of dinner to witness this breathtaking sight. That's when I know that the Island's magic has taken over—and I don't have to worry about the weekend anymore.

Saturday is sunny and breezy all day. By six o'clock we are all seated in white folding chairs on a corner of the property facing the shimmering sea. John Alley, a tall, bearded justice of the peace who has performed over a thousand weddings on the Island, presides in top hat and tails, looking very Lincolnesque. At the end of the ten-minute ceremony, he recites an ancient Apache wedding prayer:

Now you will feel no rain,
For each of you will be shelter to each other.
Now you will feel no cold,
For each of you will be warm to each other.
Now there is no loneliness for you:
There is no more loneliness.
Now you are two persons
But there is one life before you.
Now go to your dwelling place
To enter into the days of your togetherness.
May your days be good and long upon the earth.

We are all touched as the words, simple and timeless, drift over us on the gentle summer wind. It's a precious Vineyard moment—and then it's time to celebrate. After all the planning and worrying, this wedding has taken on a life of its own.

On Sunday morning a hot summer sun prevails. I sit with the Rowdy Crew on the patio of Teke and Kristie's rental behind the Allen Farm. Blue-and-white-checked tablecloths dot the tables; the comforting smell of freshly brewed coffee wafts on the breeze as we wait for brunch guests to arrive. Nearby on the farm, sheep bleat in the warm, muggy air and horses wander through the fields. Guinea hens flutter in the hedges; a late-rising rooster crows his blessing. In the distance across the rolling hills, waves break on a sliver of beach; sailboats flutter near the horizon line like tiny white butterflies.

I close my eyes and bask in the sunshine, the highlights of the weekend blurring pleasantly in my mind: sunlight and squall, a double rainbow, a mesmerizing Apache prayer. I'm winding down; I'm coasting; I'm full of contentment.

I'm winding down; I'm coasting; I'm full of contentment.

6. UNEXPECTED GIFTS / 2000

With the wedding behind me I've managed to carve out four days to focus on my writing at the Chilmark Writing Workshop. Despite ongoing weekly classes at the Writing Institute at Sarah Lawrence College, recently I've been blocked. My family memoir, *The Power of The Place*, is languishing on my desktop. I know I will have to write spontaneously at the workshop and then read my words aloud, and I'm worried. Will I be paralyzed, or will my pen fly across the page?

Lisa, now forty-two, has returned to the Island from Pittsburgh to attend the workshop with me. My daughter is the director of Gateway to the Arts, a nonprofit arts-in-education organization there, whose mission—to bring all the various arts into the public schools—she is passionate about. She is looking forward to getting away from the administrative writing that consumes her at work.

For four consecutive days from nine o'clock in the morning until noon, we sit with two men and six other women under a pine tree on rusty metal lawn chairs. Nancy Slonim Aronie, author of *Writing from the Heart: Tapping the Power of Your Inner Voice* and the leader of the workshop, welcomes us each day to "this sacred circle" on her property. Nancy is a tall, gangly, middle-aged brunette with friendly brown eyes and a warm, toothy grin. Her enthusiasm is infectious. Throughout the week she orders us to write about an assortment of things: "Dinner at My House—Family of Origin," "I Wasn't Invited," "A Fight in a Car," "What I Should Have Said," "Returning Things," "I'm Sorry," "Shoes." We write during the workshop and we write at home.

Me and Lisa after the ceremony on Stonewall, Teke & Kristie's wedding, July 8, 2000

Somehow, as the days progress under the pine tree, bathed in Nancy's nurturing aura—with Lisa next to me, her arm around my shoulders, and all the voices opening up around me—I'm able to break through my paralysis and tap into feelings that I can put on paper. By the end of the week I'm confident that I have reached a new level in my writing.

Now, on the last Friday of July, I'm alone in the house on Stonewall Beach, looking forward to a quiet weekend. Jonathan—who returned to his job in New Jersey after Teke's wedding—will fly in on Saturday for the weekend, help me pack up the car, and drive home with me on Monday.

Looking back, it's been a full month. Friends and family, ninety-strong, have come and gone for a wedding weekend that—sprinkled with Island magic—none of us will ever forget. The writing workshop with Lisa—just the two of us together on the Island, away from our boisterous, male-dominated family—was a special, intimate time for me. I feel so much closer to her, and so much closer to finding my true voice in my writing.

I'm sitting at the kitchen table around five in the afternoon, catching up with the mail from home, sorting the household bills, when the phone rings. It's Bo calling from New York City.

"Mom, are you sitting down?" he asks. "I have some . . . bad news."

My initial thought: He must have lost his job. But I say nothing.

Bo takes a deep breath on the other end of the line. Then he blurts out, "Mike is dead!"

Mike Bowman—my ex-husband, Bo's father, once the man of my dreams—is dead. My heart stops beating; the blood drains from my head; I feel prickly all over. A sensation of lightness passes through my body and joins Bo's words—seemingly floating in the air above me. I'm having an out-of-body experience, but I force myself back into the conversation.

"Are you all right, Bo? Are you feeling okay with this?"

He answers me immediately, without stopping to ponder my question.

"To tell you the truth, Mom, it's a relief."

Later that evening, I learn from Jonathan that when Mike's half-sister found his body in his apartment, the shower was running and the TV was on. He had been dead for at least a week. These morbid details are a chilling coda to my years of continuous giving and his relentless disintegration during our marriage. But Bo is right. It's a relief; it's a blessing; it's a gift. Mike's death has set me free.

This is not the only unexpected gift of the summer. At the Chilmark Writing Workshop I've received a precious gift from Lisa: the reaffirmation of a daughter's unwavering, enduring devotion. And also a treasured gift from our leader, Nancy Slonim Aronie: her limitless ability to release from captivity the caged birds around her, allowing the feelings in their hearts—and in my heart—to open up and soar.

It's a relief; it's a blessing; it's a gift. Mike's death has set me free.

7. THE ATTACK ON AMERICA / 2002

Almost six months have passed since September 11, 2001; rescue workers in the pit have finally reached what used to be the lobby of the South Tower, the first building to collapse. Just a few days ago, the remains of twelve more victims were pulled from the ruins—six civilians, five firefighters, and one Port Authority policeman. Five residents of our community have died in the Towers, including one of Jonathan's acquaintances; neighboring suburban towns have lost even more.

Thoughts of the Vineyard soothe my soul. I plan to return to the Island on July 1—with visits already scheduled from the six children, their various spouses and partners, my grandchildren, cousins, and friends—to the big, airy four-bedroom house overlooking the sea on Stonewall Beach where Kristie and Teke were married two years ago in July 2000. My ferry tickets have arrived in the mail, and I am already mentally packing: twelve beach towels, one beach umbrella, first-aid kit, two bathing suits, one pair white linen pants, black leggings, assorted tops, certain jewelry . . . the list goes on but it is not elaborate, since everyday life is still simpler on the Island.

Meanwhile here at home, life goes on. Driving into Manhattan for dinner or the theater, I can see the pair of phantom lights reaching for the sky just behind Ground Zero. Installed as temporary memorials, they seem weak and ephemeral compared to the mighty steel and glass structures that once loomed in the space.

"I can't fathom the evilness of all of this," I remember Jonathan saying to me on the day of the attack. Now, six months later, he and Bo, both in their thirties, talk about 9/11 as a turning point for their generation—a sudden, irrevocable loss of innocence, after years of peace and prosperity. They both describe a subtle depression that has crept into their consciousness, an edgy nervousness that haunts them as they go about their day-to-day routines respectively in Manhattan and New Jersey. Lately, they're not sure what they want to do for the rest of their lives; they're not even sure how much of their lives is left.

I know that I'm eating and drinking a little too much these days—it eases the sadness and anxiety. I no longer feel protected by what I've always thought of as the most powerful, most secure country in the world. Instead uncertainty and dread prevail. The invincibility of this nation is now an illusion; my cozy home in this tranquil, leafy suburb—just twenty miles from Ground Zero—no longer feels safe.

Yet I'm looking forward to my first full day on Stonewall. After the car is completely unpacked and everything is in place for the month, I'll stash my unread *New Yorkers* and a beach towel in my tote bag, grab my flowered umbrella, and walk down the pebbly path across the stones to the silky sand near the water. I won't sit too far down the beach; I love to watch the passing parade. All shapes and sizes of summer folk will come chatting through the dunes—singles and pairs and whole families; tanned, lithe teenagers; and tiny tots waddling behind mothers and fathers and grandparents. Everyone will look happy—as if they're about to discover something new. By mid-afternoon, brightly colored umbrellas will dot the sand like confetti as far as the eye can see, framed by a cloudless cerulean sky.

In the meantime, during these worrisome times here at home in New Jersey—with July still a few months away—I keep reminding myself of all the reasons I come back to the Island year after year: For the simplicity of savoring one day at a time. For living off the bounties of land and sea. For the sheer beauty of the place. For the tranquil tempo of small-town life. For the serenity that comes with getting closer to nature. For the reassurance that there is order in the universe.

And this year, the first summer after the attack on America—with the World Trade Center reduced to a pile of smoking junk and thousands of bodies pulverized in the rubble—it beckons more than ever.

Bo and Jonathan on Quansoo, August 1987

I keep reminding myself of all the reasons I come back to the Island year after year.

8. ANOTHER RIPTIDE / 2005

We're together again in Chilmark for another July reunion. Some of us gather on Stonewall Beach for an afternoon of swimming and sunning. My newest grandson, Cruz—Kristie and Teke's first child, now a year-old toddler—gingerly digs his toes into the velvety sand at the water's edge. It's low tide, and the sea is as smooth as glass. My daughter, Lisa—his godmother—takes his tiny hand in hers and coaxes him in, lifting him up in her arms for a swim.

Cruz is not the only new member of our family—although he is the youngest one. Lisa has finally met her match and has married Dr. Attilio "Buck" Favorini, the chairman of the Theatre Arts Department at the University of Pittsburgh. "When we met, I took one look at those china blue eyes and heard that bubbly laughter and I was a goner," Buck loves to tell me.

My son Jim has also started a new life. A few years ago, while his marriage to Carol was unraveling, he accidentally reconnected (via email that he thought was spam) with his childhood sweetheart, Pam—who was living with her three children forty-five minutes away from his home in Los Angeles. He and Pam are planning to marry and have rented their own house in Menemsha for the month. She is thrilled to be back on the Vineyard, having fallen in love with it on visits some years ago.

Watching Lisa and Cruz from my beach chair, my mind wanders back to May 2004, when Lisa and Buck were overflowing with joy at their wedding; they were still euphoric when they returned to Pittsburgh after a two-week honeymoon in Sicily. A few days later, Lisa called me at home in New Jersey.

Lisa and Buck's engagement photo, 2004

"I got some worrisome news today." I could hear the tension in her voice, followed by a deep breath. "I've got breast cancer."

I remember how my heart stopped beating before I burst out crying. "This was supposed to happen to me!" I exclaimed between sobs.

Both my mother and my grandmother had mastectomies; despite all precautions, I'd been waiting for years to be next.

Lisa had discovered a lump in her left breast a few weeks before the wedding but had told no one, vowing not to let it interfere with the happiest weeks of her life so far. On her return from Sicily, a mammogram and biopsy revealed a malignant tumor. A lumpectomy followed by chemotherapy and radiation were prescribed.

Forty-one years after her near-drowning off Squibnocket Beach, Lisa and I are caught up in another riptide. Once again I'm overwhelmed with panic and helpless to save her. This time we're in uncharted waters. Safety on shore is again uncertain and in the far distance. Instead of her mother, her new husband will be at her side, guiding her through the brutal battering that her body and mind will have to endure for survival. There's a 95 percent cure rate for this kind of breast cancer, we're told, if she follows the dictates of her medical team.

Six months later, when we gather in Dallas for Thanksgiving at Kristie and Teke's, the chemo sessions have taken their toll; Lisa has lost all her long, silky dark brown hair. "And not just the hair on my head," she reminds me. "All my hair." She is still beautiful, but it's the pale, gaunt beauty of a cancer victim. She has bought two wigs. "One for work and one for fun," she tells me. Amazingly, she hasn't missed a day in her office.

By Christmas the chemo has dealt its final blow; Lisa is in the throes of premature menopause. Then in January 2005, with the chemo sessions behind her and radiation treatments starting, a fierce depression takes over. An antidepressant helps diminish both the depression and also the severe hot flashes and bouts of sweating that have prevented her for weeks from sleeping through the night.

In March, when we meet in Manhattan to consult with a renowned oncologist for a second opinion, Lisa's hair has started to grow back and she has discarded her two wigs. In the waiting room, she confides her feelings to me.

"Remember the bride who walked down the aisle last May? She's gone forever.

I'll never be that person again. Even my eyelashes are different."

Now, just a few months later, Lisa's bubbly laughter interrupts my reverie on Stonewall Beach. I watch her in the water, smiling and cooing at her godson. Her dark brown hair has grown back: thick, short, and curly. "Chemo hair," she calls it. In a year it will be thick, long, and straight—as it was on her wedding day fourteen months prior. She and Buck are joyful again, and my feelings of panic and helplessness have dissipated. The perilous currents of the past year are receding in my mind.

Back in the house, from the windows of my second-story corner bedroom, the ocean spreads away, as far as my eyes can see, to the gentle curve of the horizon. Each day for the rest of my July stay, I'll watch the sun rising in the east over Cape Cod and setting in the west over the Chilmark hills. At dawn, without fail, I'll listen to a resident bobwhite greeting the light with its whistling call, and at dusk, a faithful whip-poor-will chanting its loud, namesake song. Upon sleeping and waking I'll hear the sigh of the surf—as the tides, pulled by the moon, constantly ebb and flow. Once again, the Island will continue to reassure me—as it has every summer—that despite everything, there is still order in the universe.

Once again, the Island will continue to reassure me—as it has every summer—that despite everything, there is still order in the universe.

Saturday Mornings

On Saturday mornings at the farmers' market, Lisa and I bypass the Vietnamese family at the first stall—the line is too long. We'll hit them on the way out, taking their delectable cold vegetable rolls with hoisin sauce home for a special lunch. As we pass by their counter we notice they've added blueberry tarts, meringues, and brownies to their Asian repertoire—surprise desserts, we agree, for our family dinner. / Strolling from vendor to vendor we stock up for a few days: homemade muffins and jams for breakfast, salsas and pestos to accompany fish and pasta, a special fruit pie or two for dessert. The blueberries, big as marbles, are selling out quickly, but we're not worried—the farm is not far from Stonewall and we can order them by phone. / Up and down the aisles, everyone looks happy; even the sleeping babies in their strollers and the carefully leashed dogs seem to be smiling. Just before we're finished, we can't resist a huge bouquet of Island flowers—cadmium yellow sunflowers with mossy black centers, snapdragons in hues of raspberry and lavender, daylilies from the palest cream to deep cantaloupe, blue and white hydrangeas as round as snowballs. The palette of colors takes my breath away. / On our way to the car, we bury our faces over and over again in the soft petals and summer scents. / Savor this moment, I tell myself. This is joy on the Vineyard.

9. MENEMSHA DINING / 2006

Here in New Jersey the holidays are over; Christmas and New Year's—and visiting family members—have come and gone. The tree is down, and the last stray ornament has been put away in my Christmas cupboard. As the temperatures drop into the teens, the winds whistle around the eaves of my three-story Victorian house. A winter robin pecks at the frozen water in the birdbath on my terrace. The bleak, blustery weather carries the bitter smell of approaching snow in the air.

The days are still short, and nature is at its lowest ebb. It's still too early in January to book my ferry reservations. But this is the time of year when I start to daydream about summer days on the Vineyard.

I plan to arrive on the Island the afternoon of July 1, and this year neighbors of mine

are driving up with their teenage son and daughter that same day. Mary and Roger lived abroad for over fifteen years—first in Wales, then Spain, then Holland for nine years, where Liz, now sixteen, and Andrew, now fourteen, attended local schools and learned to speak fluent Dutch. They returned to the States four years ago to give their kids an American secondary school education.

Last summer they spent a long weekend with me in my rental house in Chilmark on Stonewall Beach. All four of them fell in love with the Island, and this year they've rented a cottage just up the road from mine for the first week of July.

We'll be looking for each other in the line at Woods Hole, and we've already decided what we're going to share for dinner together on our first evening on the Island. Mary and I will take a break from unpacking and drive over to Menemsha together for some of our favorite takeout.

My mind wanders back to another dinner a few years ago, not in Menemsha, but at Menemsha—a recently opened restaurant in Marina Del Rey, California. I was visiting my son Jim and daughter-in-law Carol, who at the time lived in the Hollywood Hills. They were married on the Vineyard in July 1994 and visited me every summer in Chilmark. When we heard about this little piece of the Island in Los Angeles County, we knew we had to try it.

We spotted the sign outside the restaurant: "Menemsha" in black lettering, accompanied by a red-and-white-striped lighthouse. "Uh-oh," I said to Jim in a critical tone. "Mistake number one. Menemsha doesn't have a lighthouse, and there are no striped lighthouses on the Vineyard."

Inside the restaurant, we walked past an impressive raw bar. The chalkboard above it advertised littlenecks, cherrystones, and oysters from both Atlantic and Pacific waters. Pine paneling, brass shipboard lighting fixtures, and lobsters cavorting in a tank gave the dining room a casual, nautical feel.

The only artwork was a huge, handsome photograph of the Gay Head Cliffs. I looked at the remaining bare walls. Where were the rusty old swordfishing boats lining the Menemsha dock, the weather-beaten cottages, the famous sunsets?

The friendly, young restaurateur/owner introduced himself, explaining that his roots went back to childhood summers on the Vineyard. I admired the photograph, then pointed to the remaining bare walls. "Where's Menemsha?" I asked.

"We're working on it," he assured me. The restaurant had opened only a few weeks before; not everything was in place.

The kitchen was up and running, however, and we perused the menu, ordering wine and appetizers. Proust had his tea and his madeleines; I had my Russian River Chardonnay and my farm-raised Martha's Vineyard oysters. The memories came flooding back; nostalgia was setting in for the real Menemsha.

During my month on the Island I drive over to the quaint fishing village at least three or four times a week; it's only a couple of miles from my rental property. Sometimes I go to the sweet little beach that faces Vineyard Sound for a sunbath and a swim—the water there is the coldest on the Island. Or to get gas for my car—Menemsha Texaco is the only service station way up-Island. Or to pick up a slab of freshly caught swordfish at the Menemsha Fish Market for a family dinner. But most of the time I drive there for takeout.

My favorite meal comes from The Galley in two parts: (1) creamy white clam chowder, dotted with bits of potato and fresh quahog; (2) a lobster roll consisting of a New England frankfurter bun, slit open on top, filled first with a lettuce leaf, then a dab of mayonnaise, then several large chunks of briny, fresh lobster meat. We rush home to eat on my deck overlooking the ocean, or sometimes sit on The Galley's back porch at communal picnic tables, overlooking Menemsha Creek.

At Marina Del Rey's Menemsha the chowder was smooth and slightly spicy; one gigantic oyster cracker floated on top. My lobster roll—the bits of lobster generously laced with a mayonnaise dressing—was accompanied by delicately fried onion rings and a dollop of coleslaw. Everything was delicious, but something was missing. The culinary interpretations were elegant and sophisticated, but not authentic Menemsha.

My grandchildren Cruz and Pilar at home in Dallas, December 2008

My houseguests on the Vineyard love The Bite, where the fried clams—considered the best on the East Coast—are tightly packed into paper containers. Here, too, we eat alfresco, at picnic tables outside The Bite's kitchen—sometimes in our bathing suits—using our fingers to dip each clam lavishly into a little plastic cup of tartar sauce before munching away on the dark brown, crumbly batter coating the tender bellies inside. In Marina Del Rey the clams, arranged on plates, were pale and golden, delectably crunchy and tender. But they just didn't look right. And we had to eat them with silverware!

When we got to the temping desserts, we applauded the West Coast chef for his Yankee accents—Blueberry Buckle, Boston Cream Pie,

Indian Pudding. But where was The Galley's soft ice cream?

Two easily recognizable Hollywood couples, LA residents and also Chilmark homeowners, were sitting a few tables away. I couldn't hear what they were saying, but judging from the amply laden trays whizzing by, they, too, were eating their way down the menu, comparing and contrasting just as we were. I wondered how many Los Angelenos would come to the restaurant hoping to revive summer memories, and how many others would dine there, never having been to the Island. If so, maybe they would be inspired to travel to our pure and simple Menemsha. Perhaps after dining in Marina Del Rey's Menemsha they would be disappointed if they did actually visit our quaint, old fishing village and sample our food.

This year on July 1 in the late afternoon, Mary and I will place our order at The Galley for clam chowder and lobster rolls, then drive around the corner to The Bite for containers of fried clams accompanied by extra tartar sauce. Back at their rental house, Roger will have chilled Chardonnay waiting. We'll sit on the porch with their two kids, unwinding from our life back in New Jersey, soaking in the breathtaking view along the jagged shoreline toward Squibnocket, the Gay Head Cliffs rising in the far distance.

The soft ice cream will have to wait until a lazy afternoon later in the month. I'll park at the Menemsha Market to pick up the *Gazette* or the latest *New Yorker*, then amble down to The Galley to order my "combo" cone with sprinkles on top, watching intently as the velvety chocolate and vanilla swirl together out of the machines. I'll sit on a flat rock near The Arabella, licking away at my striped, icy tower, as happy and carefree as a child. A light breeze will be wafting off Menemsha Bight, and in the distance the Chilmark hills will be silhouetted in the summer haze.

Yes, this is the time of year that I start daydreaming about the Vineyard. . . .

A light breeze will be wafting off Menemsha Bight, and in the distance the Chilmark hills will be silhouetted in the summer haze.

10. A BITTERSWEET JULY / 2006

Six months later on a Friday morning, as I'm paying for a pile of *Vineyard Gazette*s at the Chilmark Store, a man waiting quietly behind me in line suddenly asks, "Why are you buying so many copies of today's paper?"

I turn around and recognize Peter Simon, who had photographed my son Jim's wedding on the Island in 1994.

"Because you and I are in the paper together on the commentary page, Peter!" I exclaim, opening a copy to show him.

The editors have given my essay an intriguing headline: "Halcyon Days, Bittersweet This Summer." Peter's photograph of a glowing sunset over Menemsha harbor, banked with ominous clouds, accompanies my story, which I had written and submitted from home in June.

The photo reflects the tone of my essay perfectly. In it I describe returning to the beauty and tranquility of the Island for my twentieth consecutive July. But this summer, I explain, unlike previous ones, my anticipated halcyon days will be different, with dark shadows on the horizon.

A few months earlier, my seventy-one-year-old brother, Tommy, had been diagnosed with Parkinson's disease. Growing up on "The Place," we had been inseparable, but over the years we had not sustained a close relationship. Nevertheless, he was my only sibling, two years younger than me, and we shared many memories.

Tommy was managing to get around at home in Connecticut on a walker, but in early May, while he and Connie, his wife of forty-four

On the deck at Stonewall, July 2007

years, were visiting their daughter near Boston, he collapsed and went into full cardiac arrest. The EMTs brought him back, but he has been hospitalized there ever since. He is in an extremely weakened state; he cannot get out of bed or sit and stand on his own, and can speak only in a barely audible whisper. Hopefully, with the help of physical therapy, he will become strong enough to be transported to a rehab not far from his house, but I'm worried that he will never be able to live at home again.

My brother is not the only tall oak who has fallen over the winter months. One of my best friends on the Island, married for sixty-one years, retired from the Midwest to Edgartown with her husband ten years ago. Now eighty-two, after collapsing at home and being taken to Martha's Vineyard Hospital, he was transported off Island—initially to a rehab center and recently to a nursing home in Falmouth for more intensive treatment. My friend has spent the last few months commuting from the Island by ferry several times a week to visit him. She hopes that he will return to the Island sometime over the summer, but when I call her to check on his progress, her voice is thick with tears. "Even if he comes

back," she tells me, "he may never walk on his own again."

I'm still tall, strong, and healthy, but it's all left me feeling a bit wobbly inside. I can't help thinking, When will it be my turn? This isn't the first time I've faced my own mortality; at seventy-three I've been aware for a while that there are many fewer years ahead of me than behind. But right now life seems more fragile than ever, and I'm feeling more vulnerable than before. I keep wondering, What's in store for me? And when?

Here on the Island this month, I'm trying to slow way down and take life one day at a time—some days, maybe one hour at time. And if I stop, look, and listen—really listen—maybe I'll learn something new and miraculous this bittersweet July.

I drive home to New Jersey on the first of August; by the end of the month my friend's husband has died. Twelve days later my brother dies. September 2006 turns into a month of funerals.

As the year draws to a close and the sadness abates, I start thinking back to my days on the Island this past July. I can't rationally explain why Peter Simon and I converged at precisely the same time at the Chilmark Store. It was a serendipitous moment for me—one of many that occur on the Vineyard but rarely back in my own world.

Next July 2007 will be our twenty-first consecutive summer on the Vineyard. During these past two decades, I realize that a number of ongoing magical moments— little "miracles"—have punctuated the predictability of my everyday life on the Island. These heartwarming happenings are totally unexpected and also infrequent, occurring for the most part every few years. Some of them are natural phenomena: the sea of wildflowers at Jim and Carol's wedding, the double rainbow at Teke and Kristie's rehearsal dinner. Some are quirky encounters: meeting Peter Simon in line at the Chilmark Store. Some are more spiritual: the Apache prayer that drifted over us on the summer breeze at the end of Teke and Kristie's ceremony. I've decided to collect these ongoing magical Island moments in my memory bank, savor them in my mind, then shape them into written words on paper—hoping to bring them alive in this book for Vineyard lovers everywhere.

I realize that a number of ongoing magical moments—"little miracles"— have punctuated the predictability of my everyday life on the Island.

11. ISLAND MIRACLES / 1998

Everywhere I go on my errands this July morning—to the Chilmark Store for the newspaper, to Beetlebung Farm for freshly picked lettuces, to the post office for stamps—people are buzzing about the strange catch at Poole's Fish Market in Menemsha.

When I get back to my rental house on Quitsa Lane, I share the news with my visiting family from Vermont—my oldest son, Derrik (who no longer uses his childhood name of Ricky); his wife, Margie; and my three young grandchildren, Jasper, Jovi, and Sheyna.

"Guess what? There's a blue lobster over at Poole's!" I exclaim.

Derrik, a musician and singer/songwriter, bursts out laughing. "Only on the Vineyard," he comments. Then he smiles to himself. "Once in a blue lobster," I hear him say under his breath. I wonder if a new song is in the making.

After lunch, we drive over to Menemsha to take a look. Sure enough, a one-and-a-quarter-pound chicken lobster the color of lapis lazuli is nestled in the bottom of the tank, glowing like a jewel among its sinister black contemporaries. Not only is the lobster a deep cobalt blue, but the feathery edge of its tail is bright yellow.

This rare crustacean was caught by a fisherman from New Bedford. At first, the Pooles thought that he had colored the lobster and was playing a joke. It turns out, however, that blue lobsters have shown up in the past; but according to marine biologists this mutation occurs about once in 30 million lobsters. For me and my family, however, the catch is much more than a biological phenomenon. This is quintessential Island magic, and certainly belongs on my growing list of Island "miracles."

Derrik and Margie after their wedding ceremony, June 18, 1988

A few years later, on a lazy, hazy afternoon, I drive from my Chilmark rental house on Stonewall Beach to Elizabeth Pickett's red barn on South Road—now converted into a beauty salon—for my July pedicure. When I enter the wide, open doors, I find Elizabeth looking up at the loft, making peculiar chirping noises with her tongue.

Suddenly a long pointy nose and two beady eyes ringed in black appear between the banisters. "Meet Ringo, my baby raccoon," she says to me, blowing kisses in the air toward the animal. She tells me that she found him a few months earlier on Middle Road, whimpering over the dead body of his sibling, who had been run over by a car. "He was tiny

[76]

and starving—he had no teeth and must have still been nursing when his mother for some reason abandoned him."

Soon I'm settled in a comfortable chair outside on the deck, my feet soaking in a plastic tub of soothing warm water. Before long, little Ringo, plump and furry, the picture of health, comes padding out from the barn. He stops to sniff and taste my footbath, and then becomes fascinated by my feet—rubbing them with his nose and delicately patting them with his front feet, which had long, webbed fingers and paws as soft as velvet. "Raccoons have poor eyesight," Elizabeth explains. "They depend on smell and touch."

Having befriended my toes, Ringo suddenly hops into the tub and plops himself down in the water, curling up in a corner. He's a sweet, gentle soul, and I can see why Elizabeth has become so attached to him. I, too, am entranced. But Ringo soon becomes restless, and I watch him scamper into the garden to investigate certain shrubs. Then he climbs up the trunk of a nearby leafy tree and settles onto a branch above my head to finish the morning nap that Elizabeth had interrupted in the loft upon my arrival.

"He won't be with me too much longer," she said. "Raccoons are nocturnal creatures. He's out all night and sleeps all day. Pretty soon he'll go out one night and not come back— he'll stay in his natural habitat." I could already hear the loss in Elizabeth's voice.

———

A few weeks later, Elizabeth confirmed that Ringo had returned permanently to his tribe in the wilds of Chilmark.

The cobalt blue lobster with the yellow tail was shipped to the Woods Hole Aquarium to fascinate visitors from near and far.

And over the years, I've learned that I can get by on these magical moments.

And over the years, I've learned that I can get by on these magical moments.

12. MORE ISLAND MIRACLES / 2007

In mid-July an intriguing headline appears in the *Vineyard Gazette*: "Immense Lobsterzillas Create Splash at Menemsha Fish Market." When I drive over for a look, three lobsters, two weighing eighteen pounds and one weighing nineteen pounds—caught on George's Bank by boats out of New Bedford—are snoozing in the bottom of the tank. Their claws are immense; their legs as thick as human fingers, and their antennae over a foot and a half long. They take up most of the tank, while smaller lobsters crawl around them and move about. Each one is close to (if not more than) a hundred years old.

According to the Guinness Book of Records, the largest lobster ever caught—in 1977, off the coast of Nova Scotia—weighed over forty-four pounds. Stanley Larsen, owner of the Menemsha Fish Market (formerly Poole's) and Chilmark's shellfish constable, says the way to tell a lobster's age is to count six or seven years per pound. Another method of calculation is to multiply the lobster's weight by four and then add three. He also confirms that these huge lobsters are edible and will make a delicious meal, but like a turkey or a roast, if overcooked they turn out dry and chewy. A couple from New York City has already shown interest in bringing one back for a special dinner party.

A few days later, on a calm, sunny afternoon, I'm setting the dining room table, occasionally glancing up at the breathtaking view along the jagged shoreline toward the Squibnocket cliffs and beyond. There will be more than twenty of us this evening for dinner;

The Rowdy Crew on the deck at Stonewall, July 2006

we'll be spilling out to the kitchen island and the picnic table on the deck. Suddenly something strange catches my eye across the lawn, at the edge of the property where the thick brush surrounds Stonewall Pond. It resembles a dark brown rock, but there has never been a rock there before. Then it starts to move, slowly morphing into a huge snapping turtle. Like the giant lobsters in Menemsha, it's an awesome sight—almost two feet long, leathery and lumbering, with a look of scary intensity in its beady eyes.

I phone my neighbor/landlord who lives directly across the lawn in a cottage on the pond. "There's a great big turtle heading straight for the house!"

"Not to worry," he assures me. "She comes out every once in a while to lay her eggs."

It turns out that the peak laying season for snapping turtles is June and July, and this female snapper has come out of its natural habitat—the brackish water of Stonewall Pond—to excavate a hole in sandy soil and deposit anywhere from twenty-five to eighty eggs. She will not provide any care for her babies; instead she will return to the water after laying her eggs on land. The eggs and hatchlings are frequently eaten by crows, raccoons, skunks, and other wildlife. But those that survive will find their way to a nearby pond and live as long as thirty years.

Fortunately I choose not to venture out on the lawn in order to get up close and personal with my passing visitor. Later I learn that snappers are noted for their pugnacious dispositions when out of water. They are aptly named; with a beaklike jaw and a highly mobile head and neck, this species of turtle can snap with amazing power and speed, easily biting off a human finger or toe.

I suppose a marine biologist would classify twenty-pound lobsters and two-foot-long snapping turtles as natural phenomena. But being a romantic at heart, I'm adding them to my list of Island "miracles," along with—among others—the sea of wildflowers; the cobalt blue lobster; the double rainbow; and the baby raccoon, friendly as a kitten, that eventually disappeared into the Chilmark hills, never to be seen again.

As I continue to prepare for dinner, my Stonewall snapper veers off around the house; I never see her again either. That evening, I'm surrounded by the shiny, sunburned faces of some of my children, their various partners, and assorted grandchildren, step-grandchildren, and special friends—together again from all over. The wine and the Pellegrino are flowing. Our plates are laden with the bounty of the Island—harpooned swordfish from Larsen's, Pesto Vineyardo and homemade breads from the farmers' market, organic greens from Beetlebung Farm, freshly baked fruit pies from the Chilmark Store, Chilmark Chocolates from the shop nearby on South Road. Most of us have weathered the ups and downs of another year; we're toasting each other, laughing and sharing. And I suddenly realize I'm witnessing the greatest miracle of all, for me, this summer of 2007.

Most of us have weathered the ups and downs of another year.

The Crossing

Sailboats and powerboats flirt with my four o'clock ferry as it steams toward the Island from Woods Hole. It's only a forty-five-minute trip across Vineyard Sound, but once again—as on all previous crossings—as soon as I get up on deck and settle myself in the open air, I feel all the stress draining out of my body from my hectic life back at home. / When plump seagulls hover above the railings, anticipating snacks from passengers, I know the Island is near. As soon as the huge boat nuzzles into its ferry slip, I'm ready to head out in my station wagon through the streets of Vineyard Haven. I turn off the air conditioning and lower the windows for the twenty-minute drive to my July home-away-from-home in the hills of Chilmark. Rambling roses are in full bloom on fences and doorways as I drive through the outskirts of town on my way up-Island. / Soon I pass Alley's in West Tisbury, "dealers in almost everything," where hula hoops are featured as the buy of the day on the chalkboard outside the front door. Tom Maley's whimsical sculptures frolic on the lawn of the Field Gallery across the street. On my way toward Beetlebung Corner on South Road, the scents of honeysuckle and new-mown hay drift through the open windows of the car. I drive by the Allen Farm, where horses still wander freely through the fields and roly-poly sheep still bleat at their lambs in the warm, muggy air. In the distance, beyond the rolling hills, a stretch of sea glistens in the sunlight. / I'm still a few miles from my turnoff to Stonewall, but I slow down to drink in these views that I haven't seen for a year. This is the essence of the Vineyard for me. This is the Island landscape—with its sights and sounds and smells—that I carry in my mind all winter long.

13. HEARTBREAK / 2008

It's the Fourth of July weekend; I've returned for the ninth year to the house on Stonewall Beach. At dinner Sunday evening, all my visiting older children seem mellow—opening up, sharing, and bonding. It seems to be a special time for reminiscences and revelations. I'm looking forward to the arrival of my sons Bo and Jonathan the following week. As I drift off to sleep later that night, I'm thinking that so far this is the best summer we've ever had.

The first worrisome phone call comes the following morning. Bo has been ill all weekend in New York City with excruciating pain in his left calf, flulike symptoms, and an intestinal upset. His domestic partner, Andy, is on the phone from the emergency room at St. Luke's–Roosevelt Hospital, where Bo has been taken

by ambulance from their apartment on West Sixty-Ninth Street nearby.

Bo is a gifted makeup artist; his dream is to start a makeup line of his own for women of color. He is also a runner and goes to the gym religiously; he takes good care of himself. By noon he has been sent home on crutches. Diagnosis: Intestinal flu and also a muscle pull in his leg.

Andy calls again the next morning. Bo is feeling worse and has been to see his internist, who has sent him to St. Vincent's emergency room. "They're looking for a blood clot," Andy tells me, his voice tense.

The phone calls from Andy continue every few hours throughout the day—each one more dire and terrifying than the next.

"They're still looking for blood clots."

"They're taking him into surgery."

"The doctors are mystified."

"They may do open-heart surgery."

"They may have to amputate his leg if he pulls through."

By late afternoon—with fear and uncertainty in the air—we turn to food and drink, sipping wine at the kitchen island as Jim and Pam prepare dinner; Teke serves Cruz, now almost four, his mac-and-cheese supper. In the morning, the two of them will return to Dallas—where Kristie has stayed home with Pilar, a squirmy toddler not yet ready for long-distance airplane travel. Derrik and Margie are also on hand with my granddaughter Sheyna, who starts Bennington College in the fall.

Only seven of us are at the table this evening; Lisa and Buck have already returned to Pittsburgh. We have forsaken our usual regimen of pasta or fresh fish. Instead Jim is grilling cotes de boeuf—double-cut, bone-in rib-eye steaks—while Pam puts together her version of a smashed potatoes recipe from a famous Napa chef. Freshly picked lettuces, already thrice-washed at the nearby organic farm, are ready to be tossed; a fruit pie is warming in the oven.

Andy calls again. This time there is terror in his voice. "Joan, the doctors have told me to notify the family."

I put down the phone, frozen in disbelief. I turn to everyone. "What does 'notify the family' really mean?" I ask desperately.

We are all in shock. The delicious food and wine are no longer the focus of the evening; while we eat and drink, we review the ongoing plans. Bo's younger brother, Jonathan, is already on his way to Manhattan from Denver; Lisa is flying in from Pittsburgh. Teke will fly back to Dallas with Cruz as planned early the next morning, then return with Kristie to New York to be with the family. Jim, Pam, and Sheyna are leaving the Island in two hours on a private plane to be at the hospital to join Andy during this critical night. They implore me to accompany them, but I'm adamant about not going. Sitting at the head of the table, emotionally paralyzed over the news, I embark on an elaborate bout of magical thinking: If I ignore the dire predictions from the hospital . . . if I refuse to accept that Bo is dying . . . if I stay here on my beloved Island overnight . . . if I start praying and keep on praying . . . if I get a decent sleep . . . Bo will pull through. I go to bed, hoping for a miracle. Derrik and Margie will drive me to the city early the next day.

Andy and Bo at a Brooklyn wedding, 2007

At one o'clock in the morning I'm wakened from a sound sleep. It's Andy again. Lisa is with him at the hospital. "Joan." His voice cracks. "Bo is dead. Your son is gone."

Margie and Derrik have heard the phone ring and rush in to my bedroom. We cling to each other, sobbing uncontrollably. I'm numb with shock, but briefly come to my senses. I tell Andy to insist on an autopsy. Then I collapse on my bed, with one final, sensible thought. "I don't want Teke and Cruz to hear this until they wake up. Let's all try and get some sleep."

Miraculously I sleep soundly for four hours. In the morning I'm in the kitchen sipping

black coffee, steadying myself for the trip to Manhattan ahead. I hear Teke sobbing in the upstairs hallway; Derrik must have just shared the terrible news. Then I hear adorable Cruz: "Why did Uncle Bo have to die, Daddy?"

———

On the drive to New York I think back over Bo's thirty-nine years. He was always high-maintenance—a colicky baby who slept intermittently, a hyperactive preadolescent with certain learning differences. A talented artist with his own unique vision, as a teenager he made extraordinary greeting cards that were sold in a local gift shop. In college at Sarah Lawrence—where he studied philosophy, poetry, and dance, and acted and performed stand-up comedy—there were other challenges: coming out as a gay man, a diagnosis of bipolar illness. I'm remembering all the ups and downs—but when Bo was on course he was one of the funniest, kindest, most creative people in the world. Everyone loved Bo. Why had this happened?

We learn later that he died of necrotizing fasciitis, commonly known as the "flesh-eating disease"—a virulent form of strep that usually enters the body through a cut or blister. Initially it attacks a muscle, liquefying it and often necessitating an amputation. If not caught in time, it rapidly attacks all vital organs. By the time the doctors recognized it, it was too late. Bo's kidneys failed; then his loving heart stopped beating, forever.

———

Back on the Island for the rest of my July stay I call the *Vineyard Gazette* to place an obituary. "Bo loved the Vineyard," I tell Julie Wells, the editor. I explain how he came to the Island in 1986 with seven of his classmates who had just graduated from Trinity-Pawling School. They rented a house on Church Street; he soon discovered the Vineyard Playhouse just a few doors away, joining Afterwords, an improv comedy group, and also performing in various Shakespeare productions at the Tisbury Amphitheatre over ensuing summers. He even spent a winter on the Island, during a leave of absence from college.

"Bo's friends called him a creative genius," I tell her. "He made the most extraordinary greeting cards. . . . He concocted his own gift wrappings. . . . He invented hilarious characters for his comedy routines. But his greatest gift was making everyone he came in contact with feel special. No one will ever forget his dazzling smile, his wacky sense of humor."

Julie has published a number of my essays in the newspaper in recent years. "Joan, I want you to promise me something," she entreats me at the end of our phone call. "Please write about Bo for the *Gazette*."

But I can't promise Julie anything. This summer of 2008, there are no words.

<hr />

Jonathan and Andy arrive for the last week of my rental. We stare listlessly at the sea every morning, trying to plan a celebration of Bo's life set for August 23 at the Tavern on the Green in New York City's Central Park. Condolences pour in from all over the world—by regular mail, by email, by phone. The first handwritten

note arrives in the Island mail from one of Bo's Trinity-Pawling roommates:

Bo brought so much love and joy to the world. One of my last memories of him was on the Vineyard. He insisted that Andy and I drive him to Lucy Vincent so that he could dance naked on the beach. Even though it was cold and it began to rain, this did not stop Bo. . . . Wouldn't the world be a better place if we could all just dance naked in the rain? I know Bo is doing the same in heaven.

For the first time in my Vineyard life, the Island is no comfort. The sunlight, the salt water, the summer breezes—nothing here is soothing my spirit. Birdsong at dawn and dusk is no longer reassuring. The lullaby of the tides now sounds harsh and incessant. I'm living every day in a black hole.

<hr />

Almost a year has passed. It's June 2009; in a few weeks I'll be back on Stonewall again. I still ache for Bo, but the psychic pain has diminished—it's duller, scarred over. I still weep, but I can also smile again; I can even laugh. And I can write about Bo—I've recently sent an essay about his life and death to the *Gazette*. Yet the more time that passes since that death, the more senseless it seems.

Strangely, I never dream about him or even think about him in my sleep, but every morning, upon waking, a headline immediately wraps itself around my brain: "Bo Is Dead." Nothing in my day-to-day life will ever be the same.

This July, I don't know if the Island can surprise me with the kinds of magical moments that used to lift my spirits—a sea of gaily colored wildflowers, a cobalt-blue lobster, a double rainbow. I don't know if I can be open to the magic.

This July, I don't know if the Island will reassure me—as it has every summer—that despite everything, there is some kind of order in the universe.

I do know that on the Island there's a serenity that comes with being close to nature. I know that its sheer beauty sometimes takes my breath away. I know that the tempo of life is simpler here. I can live off the bounties of land and the sea. I can savor one day at a time, even one hour at a time. I can try and live the way Bo would want me to live this first July that he's gone—here in this place that he loved beyond reason.

On the Vineyard, the moon and the stars always seem brighter and nearer to the earth. I think back to Buck's words in his eulogy at the celebration of Bo's life last August: "When you look at the stars, think about Bo. Boy, did he twinkle!"

On the first anniversary of the night that he died, I'll be on my deck near Stonewall Beach, looking up at the heavens—yearning for, reaching for, still trying in some mysterious, sacred way to touch Bo.

Wouldn't the world be a better place if we could all just dance naked in the rain?

14. A VISITATION / 2009

It appears out of nowhere on a calm, clear Saturday morning in July 2009—the largest seagull I have ever seen, with a black back and a bright orange beak. It sits motionless on the verdant front lawn of our rental house that overlooks Stonewall Beach. I call to my family—who are all getting ready for a swim—to come take a look.

We are on the Island for our twenty-third consecutive summer—my four older children from my first marriage, ages fifty-four to forty-nine, with assorted spouses, grandchildren, and step-grandchildren. My younger son from my second marriage, Jonathan, age thirty-seven, is joining us in a few days. This is our first July back since the sudden death of his brother, Bo, at age thirty-nine, from a deadly infection at St. Vincent's Hospital in New York City the previous July—2008.

Now, a year after his dying, each one of us returning to the house on Stonewall has brought shared memories of past summers with Bo and unshared fears regarding this one. This July I'm worried. The horror of his death haunts me—unexpectedly washing over me in huge waves. Will I be open to discover more "miracles" on my beloved Island that will inspire me to write? Without Bo, will the Island hold the same magic?

Suddenly the gull stands up and starts slowly hopping toward the house on one leg, its huge right wing drooping to the ground. Clearly, the bird is seriously injured. I consult with Teke and Lisa. Should we leave this giant seagull alone or try to rescue it? The three of us agree that I should make some calls.

The first one, to the local police, is fruitless.

"I'm so sorry," I'm told. "We do not rescue wounded birds here in Chilmark."

This surprises me, but I'm undaunted; I have a second plan. I immediately phone Gus Ben David, the former director of Mass Audubon's Felix Neck Wildlife Sanctuary, now the proprietor of the World of Reptiles and Birds Park in Edgartown. Gus is a third-generation Islander who grew up on a Vineyard farm; as a youngster he developed a sense of wonder and appreciation for all animals. I have never met Gus, but he is legendary, not only on the Island, but also in the world of naturalists. I know his knowledge and love of birds are profound, and I'm certain he can help us in some way. When I hear his answering machine I leave a long message.

In the meantime, the huge gull has made its way up onto our deck, then slowly and painstakingly has hopped back down onto the lawn. "Don't get too close!" I warn Teke's son Cruz, my sweet-natured, tousled-haired five-year-old grandson. "Seagulls can bite."

Within the hour, Gus calls back; I describe the gull's injuries. "There is no hope for a bird this severely wounded," he tells me. "But if you're willing to bring it to me, I will euthanize it. Otherwise, if you leave it alone, it will eventually die, probably in the bushes on your property."

Teke, Lisa, and I agree to capture the bird for the twenty-minute transport to the World of Reptiles and Birds in Edgartown. Gus has instructed me well. We find a box with a lid in the garage; Teke throws a beach towel over the bird, gathers it up, puts it in the box, and seals the lid with tape. "You don't want that gull jumping out of the box and menacing everyone while you're driving," Gus warned me.

Teke drives his van to Edgartown with me in the passenger seat, Cruz in his car seat in the back, and the seagull in his box in the way back. We can hear the bird flapping, trying to escape his cardboard confines. When we get to the Park, Gus rushes over to greet us—an energetic outdoorsman in his early sixties with salt-and-pepper hair and matching beard. He snatches the bird deftly from the box, scrutinizing it quickly before tucking it under his arm as if it were a package. "That's a Great Black-Backed Gull—the largest species of seagull. But this poor bird is nothing but feather and bone. He's starving to death—was probably injured at least three weeks ago." Then he spreads out the broken wing. "You can see how the muscle has already necrotized," he comments.

Pam and Jim at Lisa and Buck's wedding reception in New York City, May 2004

A shudder passes through my body when I hear the word "necrotized." In all my seventy-six years, I had never heard the word "necrotizing" until Bo's death. And now, only a year later, I've heard it again.

Gus whisks the bird off into his basement, then returns to show us around. Huge snakes curl around themselves in their terrariums; rare birds flutter in their cages on the property; a huge tortoise basks in his pen. Cruz is fascinated by the exotic collection, but soon it's time to head home for lunch. In the van on the way back to Chilmark all three of us are silent, turning over in our minds the events of the morning. Suddenly Cruz pipes up from his car seat behind us: "Daddy, why did the seagull have to die?"

I think back to the day of Bo's death the summer before this, when sweet Cruz asked the very same question: "Daddy, why did Uncle Bo have to die?" Then it occurs to me that for two consecutive Julys on this magical island my innocent young grandson has been brushed by death. But back at the house, he seems his usual carefree self as he sprints around the front lawn, kicking his soccer ball.

———

Returning home to New Jersey in August, ruminating on our July 2009 Vineyard stay, I'm unable to rationally explain why that gigantic, wounded bird showed up on our property on that halcyon July morning. My son Jim reminds me that numerous myths have linked birds to the journeys undertaken by human souls after death. Birds also appear in Hindu mythology as symbols of the soul or as forms taken by the soul between earthly lives. The Greeks and Celts believed that the dead could reappear as birds. I would like to believe that there was some kind of connection between that visiting seagull and Bo. If not, why were we so intent on rescuing it?

A few months later, during one of our weekly Sunday morning phone calls, I ask Lisa and Teke for their recollections of "the day of the seagull." "That was so bizarre," Lisa tells me. "In all the years we've been coming to the Island, we've never before encountered an injured animal." Teke finds it "eerie and disturbing . . . the timing so poignant just two weeks after the first anniversary of Bo's death."

Now three years have passed, and the summer of 2012 is approaching. A friend of mine who knew and loved Bo tells me that his spirit is all around us, even if we don't recognize it, touching us in different ways.

Since our adventure with the wounded seagull in 2009, however, I haven't found any signs of him again on the Island—or anywhere else for that matter. He never appears in my dreams either.

But I can still recall in a flash that unique charisma that drew people to him—his wild, witty exuberance; his gorgeous, beckoning smile. I still remember how his kindly spirit touched so many lives.

And I still miss him terribly. Every day.

I still remember how his kindly spirit touched so many lives.

15. JOYOUS MEALS / 2012

I'm reading from my family memoir, *The Power of The Place*, to a group of senior citizens in the multipurpose room of their community center. About thirty older people—men and women—are listening attentively. Off to the side, I notice a middle-aged black woman sitting on a bench in front of a baby grand piano.

I describe the formal dining room, where my grandfather's gilt-framed portrait above the mantel was complemented by hand-painted Chinese wallpaper, shiny mahogany furniture, and a pewter chandelier. Under the table, a little brown box allowed my mother, at the touch of a toe, to summon Margaret, our downstairs maid, from the adjoining pantry, when she and my father were ready for the next course from the kitchen—where Gerda, our skilled cook, presided.

Then I explain that my brother, Tommy, and I were not invited to dine with my parents under the pewter chandelier until we were teenagers. Instead we were relegated to the card room, where Margaret would bring our food from the kitchen on a large tray, and our strict Swiss governess Mamzelle would eat with Tommy and me at the bridge table. Once, at supper in the card room, when I was eight or nine years old, in an attempt to break me of the habit of sniffing Gerda's delicious food before tasting it, Mamzelle pushed my face into a bowl of beautiful, steamy green pea soup. As far as I knew, no one ever told my mother about this incident, since nothing was allowed to interfere with her "perfect" life on "The Place" with my father.

I continue to read a few more excerpts that reveal the dichotomy that existed during

My grandson Jasper and his friend Alex Rabe at the Chilmark Community Center, July 2005

my growing-up years on "The Place"—the sensuous delights surrounding me there that compensated for the emotional unavailability of my mother and father. A lively question-and-answer period follows. After an hour and a half, as I'm packing up my books and getting ready to leave, the woman from the piano bench stops by on her way out.

"I really enjoyed your presentation," she tells me. "I'm an employee here, and I love coming to these talks. This morning I learned something new. I grew up in the Deep South— we were a big family and very poor. But we always had joyous meals. I never realized until today that wealthy people weren't always happy at mealtimes."

I'm completely startled by her statement; it's a concept I've never heard before. Driving home, turning her words over in my mind, I think back to the formal, structured days of my lonely childhood, recalling again the emotional deprivation and lack of intimacy that was covered up by the sheer abundance of life on "The Place." Then I think about "joyous meals"—and soon I'm daydreaming about Martha's Vineyard.

This coming July will be our twenty-sixth consecutive summer stay there. Since that summer of 1987 on Quansoo, all my children—and assorted spouses, grandchildren, cousins, and close family friends—have managed to come for a least one long weekend. The Island always surprises and delights us, and inevitably, no matter which rental house or what year, it seems I am blessed with a month of healing and renewal.

Filling my rental house on Stonewall Beach with family and friends is similar to running a bed-and-breakfast—except that the major focus is on dinner, not breakfast. Each morning over coffee, we all decide on the menu and come up with a head count. Later, everyone goes off to do their favorite thing—sail, swim, gallery hop, shop. Then an hour or so before dinnertime, we gather around the stainless-steel kitchen island, sipping Chardonnay or Pellegrino, relating our adventures of the day while we pitch in to prepare the meal. On "The Place," the menus were planned privately by my mother each morning in conference with her cook, and the elaborate dinners were prepared by the cook alone in her kitchen—her private domain—and served formally by the downstairs maid. Here, in my kitchen on Stonewall, we're all involved. For a brief time, we've gathered together—which doesn't happen very often in a given year—to eat, drink, and be merry. We're totally absorbed in the present.

At least once a week, we order pound-and-a-half lobsters from Larsen's Fish Market in Menemsha. (One of my houseguests, however, a teenage boy, ingests a three-pounder with ease.) When we pick them up in the late afternoon they're already steamed, split, cracked, and carefully packed, each with its own tiny plastic cup of drawn butter. Sitting barefoot at the picnic table on the deck, dipping succulent chunks of lobster meat into the melted butter, flinging empty shells into the dump buckets at each end of the table as the sun sets over the Chilmark hills—it's a sensuous, liberating experience for me. Nearby, while we eat, Pilar and Cruz, my two youngest grandchildren—ages three and six—frolic on the lawn. "There's nothing like the sound of children's laughter at the end of a summer's day," my neighbor tells me. I'm remembering that, on "The Place," children were seen but not heard, and we certainly never threw lobster shells around or ate with our hands at the mahogany dining table.

Here on the Island our food is wholesome and delicious, but not the haute cuisine that emanated from the kitchen in the mansion on "The Place." My own cooking skills are self-taught and basic, and I happily relinquish my

culinary space to more creative houseguests. "The kitchen's all yours," I tell Jim, fifty-five, my second-oldest son, and Buck, sixty-five, my daughter Lisa's husband—both excellent cooks—when they visit. It means so much to me that they want to take over. We still plan the menus each morning and come up with a head count; Jim and Buck usually cook on alternate days. Jim always offers to prepare his fettuccine with clam sauce. In the late afternoon he and his fiancée, Pam, come in from grocery shopping, their brown paper bags overflowing with parsley, lemons, garlic, canned clams, fresh clams, and boxes of pasta. I love sitting in the kitchen, watching them slice and dice; I feel their happiness as they cook together.

One morning at breakfast as we start our head count for the evening meal, the numbers increase exponentially and include two vegetarians. I know I can seat ten at my dining table, eight at the picnic table on the deck, and four around the kitchen island. It happens to be Buck's turn. Buck is a professor, a Shakespeare scholar, a playwright—an erudite man who seems momentarily stymied by the challenge. "Let me think about this," he says over his coffee; by lunchtime he has his solution. "Turkey burgers for twenty-two!" he announces with glee. In the kitchen cupboard I've hidden a basket of fresh cherries and chocolate chip cookies from the Chilmark Market—they're freshly baked every morning and are as big around as a bread-and-butter plate.

This July I'll have an authentic chef in my Vineyard kitchen. My grandson Jasper, twenty-nine, has put aside four years of teaching autistic children at the New England Center for Children and is attending the Cambridge School for Culinary Arts. "I can't wait to cook for the family on the Island this summer," he tells me. "I'm planning to make fresh Danish for breakfast. . . . I've got a great turkey chipotle chili I can whip up for dinner for ten or twenty. . . . And I want to go out and catch my own fish."

It's been a long journey from the elegant dining room in the mansion in the 1930s to the picnic table on the deck at Stonewall Beach in 2012; my eightieth birthday is coming up in August. There's been plenty of heartbreak along the way—the double disillusionment of two failed marriages, the senseless death four years ago of my cherished thirty-nine-year-old son, Bo. But like the woman on the piano bench, I, too, have learned something new. I'm not quite sure how it happened, but today, the lost, lonely little girl who grew up on "The Place"—with the best of everything and the worst of nothing—is surrounded by riches of a different kind.

On the Vineyard, at the picnic table at sunset—encircled by family and friends, and giddy from the food, wine, and chatter—I'm immersed in the feeling that, at least for now, everything is right with my world—and the hope that together, every July, we will continue to create our very own joyous meals.

I'm immersed in the feeling that, at least for now, everything is right with my world.

AFTERWORD

HIDING IN PLAIN SIGHT

In July 2012, at a book signing at Featherstone Center for the Arts in Oak Bluffs, I'm introduced to Jan Pogue, the proprietor of Vineyard Stories, a publishing company on the Island. Driving back to Chilmark, my houseguest, Sheila, who is visiting from Connecticut, remarks, "You know, Joan, you should send Jan your *Gazette* articles and talk to her about putting them between covers."

This should have been a serendipitous moment for me, but for some reason, my friend's excellent advice goes in one ear and out the other. A few months later, back at Sarah Lawrence for Joelle Sanders's fall writing workshop—trying to get the creative juices flowing again—I present several rewrites of the stories to which my friend was referring.

"These are too good! You've got to publish them in a book!" both my classmates and Joelle extol me.

Apparently this book has been hiding in plain sight for some time. But finally, my stars are aligned and everything starts to click into place. I call Jan and then send her a copy of my family memoir, *The Power of The Place*, and the dozen or so essays that I have written since 1998 for the *Vineyard Gazette*, suggesting a book—incorporating all these stories and more—about the impact the Island has had on my family and me for over half a century. By January 2013 she has agreed to edit and publish my new book; Alison Shaw, a renowned Island photographer whose work I've admired for years, has read my writings and has agreed to shoot the book while I'm in Chilmark in July. We've agreed on a tentative title: *Some Kind of Lucky*.

Does it get any better than this? I keep asking myself. I only wish Bo were here to share my excitement and joy.

I will dedicate my book to him. In the meantime, I can't help daydreaming about the summer of 2014. It will be a July like no other. I can see myself with friends and family in the Island's bookshops, looking at my book on the shelves—with its magical cover photograph by Alison Shaw beckoning to potential readers. Then I think back to my first summer here fifty-two years ago—my first summer of healing and serenity—in the old sea captain's house near the Gay Head Light with my four young children. Who could have predicted this?

I have been some kind of lucky.

Joan Cowen Bowman was born in Long Branch, New Jersey, in 1932. She graduated from the Baldwin School in Bryn Mawr, Pennsylvania, in 1950 and from Smith College with Honors in English in 1954. Since 1960, she has lived in Short Hills, New Jersey, where she raised five sons and one daughter. She also attended the New York School of Interior Design and the Writing Institute at Sarah Lawrence College. In 2005, at age seventy-two, she received her MFA in writing from Sarah Lawrence.

An interior designer for the past thirty-five years, she has written a weekly column on the secrets of successful home design for a local newspaper. In 2010 she authored a family memoir, *The Power of The Place*. Her essays have been published in the *Vineyard Gazette* on Martha's Vineyard where she spends every July—joined by family and friends who come to share her day-to-day life there, close to the land and the sea.

PHOTO BY PUIMING WEBSTER

Alison Shaw is a Martha's Vineyard–based photographer who specializes in fine art and editorial photography. The island has provided the primary inspiration and subject matter for her photography.

Alison's photos grace the pages of innumerable books, magazines, and newspapers—this is her seventh book for Vineyard Stories.

The Alison Shaw Gallery, which she co-owns with her partner, Sue Dawson, is located in an old single-engine firehouse in the heart of the Arts District in Oak Bluffs. You can view more of her work at www.alisonshaw.com.

Until I Return . . .